PRESENTS

THE DEFINITIVE GUIDE TO

FORTNITE

2021

A TOTALLY INDEPENDENT PUBLICATION

Written by Naomi Berry
Designed by Chris Dalrymple

A Pillar Box Red Publication

© 2020. Published by Pillar Box Red Publishing Limited. Printed in the EU.

ISBN 978-1-912456-67-3

WELCOME

The idea that Epic Games' Fortnite was a flash in the pan has long passed. The idea that it would fall victim to certain 'Fortnite-killer' games has long passed. Here we are at the dawn of a new decade, and Fortnite is still standing - victory royale, over and over again.

Since 2017, Fortnite's island has been a place where over 350 million registered players have fought to the death in Battle Royale. The game has grown from a more cartoonish and colorful option in the battle royale genre to becoming not just dominant, but genre-defining. Fortnite is a juggernaut, one of the most popular games in the world; so unmatched that at the height of its power and popularity, the developers decided to scrap everything and start again with Chapter 2.

And that's exactly what helps Fortnite stand the test of time: its ability to keep things fresh and more importantly, keep players on their toes. There are always new updates with new content, which means there's always something new to encounter, learn and master, no matter how long you've been playing. It's never too late to be the last one standing.

This guide is aimed at players old and new - there's no one way to win at Battle Royale, so when you can learn all the elements and mechanics at hand, you can craft the path to victory that suits your playstyle best. There's a storm brewing, so best get ready.

CONTENTS

GLOSSARY

Fortnite may be on its second round, but there's no shame in reviewing the basics, especially since new game mechanics and systems have brought in new lingo to learn. It's time to expand your lexicon to truly maximize your Battle Royale prowess.

Understanding the terminology is useful for general play, but totally essential if you want to play with teammates and communicate in the most effective way possible. Here's a list of the most basic phrases you'll come across in this guide and also while playing. Hey, you can't win the battle without knowing your Ps and Qs, right?

BATTLE PASS:

A Battle Pass is an in-game purchase that is available every season. It provides the player with new cosmetics and tasks, rewarding their progress with items and V-Bucks.

BLOOM:

A weapon's bloom refers to the spray of its bullets once fired. A weapon that has bloom will fire a bullet anywhere within its crosshair, which has lower accuracy than a direct snipe. You can lower the chance of bloom by standing still or crouching while shooting.

THE BUBBLE:

The circle of the map that is unaffected by the storm. Stay safe by keeping inside the bubble.

BUSH CAMPER:

A player that uses bushes to take cover and hide.

BM:

This stands for 'Bad Manners', and is a light take on post-kill or post-win celebrations at the expense of the opponent (like breakdancing on their corpse, for example).

BOT:

A player who's playing badly, or making poor game decisions.

CHAPTER 2:

Refers to Fortnite's second phase, the new installment/update that went live in October 2019.

HEALS:

Any item that provides health points, from bandages to fish.

LAUNCH:

If a teammate says, "I have a launch", it means that they have a launch pad.

LOADOUT:

The weaponry and items you have in your arsenal. Having an ideal loadout in mind while playing will speed up the loot and cop-or-drop decision making process.

LTM:

Stands for Limited Time Mode. Developers add these special game modes to spice up gameplay for a season, or a limited event.

KNOCKED:

To 'knock' an opponent means to knock them down without fully eliminating them.

MATS:

Mats is shorthand for materials, i.e. wood, brick and metal.

MINIS:

There are a lot of mini-somethings in Fortnite, but the solo 'mini' refers to the Small Shield Potion.

NO SKIN:

A player that does not have a custom skin equipped.

ONE/ONE-SHOT:

When an opponent is 'one' or 'one-shot', it means that they are one shot away from being knocked down. This is vital communication for teammates as it can dictate whether they should rush an enemy or take cover.

POI:

An acronym for Point of Interest. On the Battle Royale map, POIs are notable locations on the island, such as Bob's Bluff, Lazy Lake, Salty Springs etc.

PVE:

Player versus Environment. This is non-online play, and is the game mode in Fortnite: Save the World.

PVP:

Player versus Player. This is online play, and is the game mode in Fortnite: Battle Royale.

REZ:

Shorthand for resurrection, usually used by players who require teammates to resurrect them.

RUSH:

To rush an opponent means to make a direct offensive push to take them out. It's risky, as it's impossible to know what loadout the enemy's playing with. Keep this move for when you're sure your opponent is weak or one-shot.

SHIELD POP:

This call means that an opponent's shield has been either partially or fully destroyed.

SPAWN ISLAND:

The area you are loaded into while waiting for the game to start. You cannot access this part of the map once the game has begun. Spawn Island regularly changes to reflect the season's theme, or tease upcoming changes.

TAG/TAGGED:

Landing or taking a hit. If someone is tagged, it means they have been hit. This can let teammates know to either finish off the kill, or help you heal up.

THE BEGINNING OF THE END...

The year was 2019, the month was October, the day was a Sunday, and the global phenomenon that is Fortnite was closing its tenth season in anticipation for its logical successor: Season 11. Only, as the days of Season 10's end grew closer, people began to realise that things seemed to be going a little differently this time - namely in the form of the island and all of its inhabitants being sucked up into an interdimensional vortex and catapulted into a black hole instead of just receiving the usual update patch notes. Where were you when Fortnite deleted itself?

WHAT WENT DOWN

It started with a simple rocket launch from the Dusty Depot, shooting directly into the sky and creating a giant rift that connected with the other rifts that had already been scattered across the island. The rocket began soaring through the rifts, wreaking havoc before creating one huge rift for a giant meteor to sail through and crash into the island.

While the event itself was cool, it wasn't totally out of the ordinary (after all, Fortnite had been getting grander and grander with its in-game events) - it was what came next that was probably the game's most ambitious storytelling move yet. Fortnite went down. Like, unplayable down. For two days. And Epic went silent.

!!!

To hype up the mystery, Epic even deleted all of the official Fortnite Twitter's tweets and wiped the game's public Trello page.

KONAMI CODE

During the black hole, if players entered the famed Konami code (↑, ↑, ↓, ↓, ←, →, ←, →, B, A, Start), it would load the Durr Burger arcade mini-game from the Chapter 1 - Season 9 trailer and the World Cup livestream.

THE BLACK HOLE

The event was officially called 'The End', and players were perplexed. There had been no announcement or information other than the presence of a giant black hole. Everything got sucked in: the island, the players, and even menu elements and UI. Obliterated.

There may have been literally nothing going on, but players were hooked. The End was one of the biggest singular online gaming events to date, with more than 7 million concurrent viewers across Twitch, Twitter and YouTube.

Dedicated viewers keeping a diligent eye on the black hole began to report mysterious numbers materializing and dematerializing just as quickly. When players assembled all the numbers together, they matched them up with words from the Visitor's audio cassette tapes from the Season 10 Overtime challenges:

> **I was not alone.**
> **Others were outside the loop.**
> **This was not calculated.**
> **The nothing is now inevitable.**

Poetic. But... huh? Did it mean Fortnite was gone for good? Was the black hole the beginning of the end? Or...

THE END OF THE BEGINNING...

After 40 hours, the black hole disappeared, and from it emerged Chapter 2 - the birth of a new beast...

THE NEXT CHAPTER

So the seasonal model went out the window with a bang - or, well, a black hole - and Chapter 2 brought the most changes the game had seen since its debut in 2017. And to add intrigue to the mounting mystery, Epic didn't even have the decency to drop some patch notes on the poor, puzzled players. So, what were the biggest changes Chapter 2 brought to the table?

A NEW ISLAND

This was the biggest change - in the past, the island was updated every season, but this was the first time a whole new island got swapped in. And what's more, when Chapter 2 dropped, the map itself was totally blank. Players had to navigate the island and map it out themselves, discovering the new and returning POIs on their way, and also discovering a whole lot of...

WATER

One of the biggest changes in the gameplay came in the form of good old H20 - and it was everywhere. Even before the grand flooding of Chapter 2 - Season 3, players were confronted with a good deal more water than before when loading up Chapter 2, with rivers, lakes and big bodies of the blue stuff making up a significant portion of the map. Water is a huge part of Chapter 2 gameplay, with motorboats, new swimming effects, and even fishing.

STREAMLINED ARSENALS

Sometimes less is more, and perhaps Epic realised that as they added the Infinity Blade back in Chapter 1 and thought, 'Where do we even go from here?' Back to basics seemed to be the answer, with about two dozen weapons wiped when Chapter 2 dropped, making Fortnite's firing fights a lot more simple.

But stripped back doesn't mean basic - Chapter 2 also introduced Upgrade Benches around the map, where players could fine tune and upgrade any weaponry they found (eliminating some of that RNG that plagued past matches).

TIP:
Curious about the new playstyles Chapter 2 has to offer? Take the Pick Your Playstyle quiz on p.30-31 to find the best one suited to you.

SUPPORT SKILLS

Guns ablaze isn't the playstyle for everyone, and if you prefer to play more of a supportive role in the battlefield alongside your buddy, Chapter 2 gives you a lot more ways to make an impact. New features like being able to carry your downed teammates out of harm's way and wielding a bandage bazooka to heal them from a safe distance makes the medic playstyle way more viable.

NEW PROGRESSION SYSTEMS

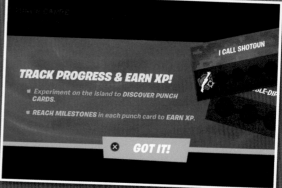

TRACK PROGRESS & EARN XP!

- Experiment on the island to **DISCOVER PUNCH CARDS**.
- **REACH MILESTONES** in each punch card to **EARN XP**.

❌ **GOT IT!**

I CALL SHOTGUN

It's easier than ever in Chapter 2 to make progress as the new experience system expands way beyond the parameters of racking up a kill count. Players can now earn experience for a myriad of gameplay things, including harvesting materials and opening chests. There's also new Medal and Punchcard systems that encourage players to carry out specific actions. Check out p. 42-43 to find out more info on making progress.

NEW STEALTH OPTIONS

Speaking of enabling different playstyles, Chapter 2 also provides a boon for those who prefer to take a more stealthy approach. Fortnite OG brought some foliage to the fight, but Chapter 2 is host to a new slew of stealth options significantly more dignified than squatting in a bush. You can now stalk your prey while using tight spaces like haystacks, barrels and dumpsters to hide in.

Stop Hiding

THE 3 BASICS:
GATHERING

There are three basic skill sets to master if you want to become the ultimate Battle Royale champion: gathering, building and surviving. Let's take a closer look at the first of those three - gathering. It's the most fundamental of all skills because if you're not gathering right, you're not building right, and you're not surviving right, and good chances are, you're not winning much either.

TOOLS OF THE TRADE

Every player is equipped with a trusty Pickaxe upon landing. It may seem like a simple hack and slash to get things going, but you should exercise some caution before swinging it around like a madman. If you hit a Treasure Chest before you open it, it'll be destroyed, along with the items within.

PICKAXE PROFICIENCY

Speed is always of the essence when it comes to improvement in Battle Royale, and gathering is no exception. To maximise your gather, aim for the Critical Point; this blue circle marks the weakest point of the mat, and striking it increases both the speed and the yield.

THE RULE OF THREE

Before you dive into either this chapter or even the island itself, you need to know that there are three categories that all materials (or "mats", as they're commonly called) fall into: wood, stone and metal.

TIP

You can hold up to x999 of each mat, so there's never any harm in stocking up if the opportunity arises. You never know when you'll need it, or how much.

WOOD

Wood is the most easily acquired of mats and the most abundant across the island, but while it's certainly the fastest mat to build with, it's also the weakest. If you're looking to source some lumber, then look no further:

· TREES:

Duh, I know, but sometimes you have to state the obvious. Trees are all across the map and can be struck down for some wood in a pinch. If you want to play like a pro, then never complete the full hack-down. Check out Pro Survival Tips on page 32 for more info!

· WOODEN STRUCTURES:

There are a number of shacks and small wooden structures dotted around the island that can be harvested for mats. You can also glean wood from the smallest of structures, like boxes, crates and even furniture.

· FENCES:

Perfect for speedy gathering, fences break down super easily and are great for some primary harvesting if you land in a residential area.

STONE

As a mat, stone is pretty much a middle-man. It comes second in both durability and build speed. If you need to find some stone, then look to:

· ROCKS:

Natural resources tend to be the most bountiful compared to structures, but rocks are a little harder to come by.

· BUILDINGS:

If it has walls, it can come down. While they're certainly abundant, they do take a while to come down, so they're not the best pick in a pinch, or if you have unexpected company.

METAL

If you're looking for a fort, then metal's got your back. It's the slowest to build with but has the highest HP of all three mat types. It's risky to whip out in the 1v1 but a must if you need to turtle down. So where can you find metal?

· VEHICLES:

All those abandoned cars and trucks along the roads have some use, and it's to provide you with around 30 metal pieces per hit. They have the highest metal payout by far, but they carry the risk of setting off the car alarm and alerting nearby players.

· METALLIC STRUCTURES:

Things that look like they were built with metal are generally good to harvest, like shipping containers, lamp posts, and some furniture.

· METAL FENCES:

These have a low pay out but come down super quickly, so are great if you need it in a pinch.

THE 3 BASICS:
BUILDING

Now that you have your mats, it's time to put them to use. Building in battle royale is a gameplay element unique to Fortnite, and while you can, essentially, play without building at all, it's an integral skill to have in your arsenal if you want to improve and play like a pro.

So why build if you don't have to? Because building is your way to manipulate the map. You can create cover, interrupt lines of sight from enemy snipers, box in an opponent, create a bridge between mountain peaks and even break your fall when you take a tumble. Being able to build is just as important as being able to aim in Fortnite, so get out your blueprints and your no. 2 pencil and get to it.

BUILD LIKE A PRO

Turbo Build is a must for quick and efficient building. It lets you hold down left-click and place structures continuously by your aim. Make sure it's enabled in your settings. If you're playing with a controller, try changing the controller config to Builder Pro.

KNOW YOUR NUMBERS

All good builders know their mats, and once you've gathered the resources from the previous chapter, you need to get familiar with their stats. We're talking minimum HP, maximum HP, seconds to reach maximum HP... It sounds a little intimidating, but it'll be second nature in no time.

Material	Structure	Min. HP	Max. HP	Secs to Reach Max. HP
Wood	Wall	90	150	4
	Ramp, Floor, Roof	84	140	3.5
Stone	Wall	99	300	11.5
	Ramp, Floor, Roof	93	280	12
Metal	Wall	110	500	24.5
	Ramp , Floor, Roof	101	460	22.5

So TL;DR - wood is flimsy but fast and best for emergencies (like negating fall damage or escaping enemies), stone isn't the best at anything so should be used as a last resort, and metal is best for long term/late game structures. Easy peasy.

TIP
Each individual structure costs 10 mats from your inventory.

THE FOUR STRUCTURES

There are four main types of structure you can build in Fortnite: the wall, the ramp, the floor and the roof.

- **The Wall:** Your first line of defence, the wall is what you should be chucking up should you find yourself under fire and without pre-made cover. It also has the most post-build editing options to create vantage points for shooting.

- **The Ramp:** This structure enables mobility and is best used for a quick escape or to gain the high ground advantage over an opponent.

- **The Floor:** A little less commonly used than the previous two, but floors are integral to provide defence when building upwards, particularly from sneaky enemies who are trying to infiltrate your build from below.

- **The Roof:** It goes without saying (but hey, we'll say it anyway) that the roof prevents enemy ambushes from above. They're also key to boxing in opponents (try throwing a trap in too for good measure).

THE ART OF EDITING

Any good artist knows that half the work is in editing, and Fortnite building is no different. Learning to edit your builds to cater to the context is a quick way to climb the ranks. Use windows to create vantage points, doors for a sneaky back exit from a frontal barrage, and partial walls for peeking and cover. True pros can edit squares of floors on the fly to create quick descents to ambush unsuspecting passing enemies or make a low-ground escape when under fire.

FOUNDATION, FOUNDATION, FOUNDATION

There are certain elements of Fortnite that definitely stray from the realm of reality (water-skiing muscle cats immediately come to mind) but something that the mechanics borrowed from our world is the importance of foundation in building.

Foundation is integral to building in Fortnite, and understanding that is the key to both optimal offence and defence when involved in a building 1v1. For any structure to stand, it has to be anchored at some point to the map, which means to take down the entire structure, you really only need to take out the foundation. So keep this in mind for the following scenarios:

- When building your own structures, try to use more than one anchor. This will reinforce your structure considerably against enemies, who will be forced to take out multiple targets in order to down your build.

- The same works in reverse when you're facing someone with a structural headstart. Don't waste time aiming at your opponent with the high-ground advantage who is continuously building; quickly source out the foundation to their structure and take it down ASAP.

- If you stumble across two players already engaged in a build fight, why not crash the party with a swift strike to their foundation while they're distracted? If they haven't already made sizable dents in each other's HP, the fall damage and shock factor certainly puts the ball in your court.

YOUR GO-TO BUILDS

So now you know your mats, your structure types and your structure stats, it's time to get building. The island is your oyster, technically, and while you can create a structure to rival the Sydney Opera House if your heart truly desires, it's best to nail the following bread and butter builds first if you prioritise a competitive edge over flair.

TIP:

Battle Royale is a pressure cooker at the best of times, let alone while you're trying to follow instructions to build your first turtle. The best place to practice building is in the Battle Lab and Creative modes. Practice makes perfect, after all.

- **1x1:** The most basic of builds, the 1x1 is four walls with a ramp in the centre for extra cover. Use this simple structure to take quick cover and consider your next move, or to ensure safety when using slower Healing items like campfires.

- **Basic Ramp:** A basic ramp is a one-layered diagonal build that can enhance your mobility. Throw one up to reach higher ground to escape or give yourself the high ground advantage. While it's a fast build, it is easy to topple due to its weakness, so it's not the best choice for super vertical routes (i.e. scale a hill, not a mountain).

- **Reinforced Ramp:** This ramp is the buffer older brother of the basic ramp, with walls and floors built beneath each individual incline. It means three structures per incline, and while it may take three times longer to build, it's also three times sturdier, which makes it three times harder for enemies to shoot through.

- **Turtle:** A turtle is essentially just a 1x1 with a roof, but the more it multiplies, the harder it becomes to crack. Building turtles next to each other and editing your path through them creates a very difficult fort for your opponent to infiltrate. They come with serious defensive power, but they require quick skills in editing and repair to truly work.

- **90s:** Ah, the 90 - a difficult beast to tame, but a wild one to have in your arsenal. The name comes from the building process, in which you need to turn continuously by 90 degrees, building up one floor per turn. This complicated build is the best when it comes to out-maneuvering your opponent and gaining quick vertical distance to get the high ground while providing a strong cover and foundation. These are tricky to pull off but invaluable - you've got to get used to simultaneous turning, jumping and building (no big deal), so try looking up tutorials on YouTube to nail the technique.

TIP:
Building in Battle Royale is a game of intuition, and you can't tap into your primal builder beast if you're fumbling over awkward key inputs. Be sure to customize your keybinds to whatever works best for you for some fast-fingered forging - sometimes the presets aren't necessarily one size fits all.

THE 3 BASICS:
SURVIVING - WEAPONS

The last of the three basics is perhaps the most difficult (nailing 90s aside), and definitely the most multi-faceted. There's really only one method of Gathering, and one method of Building, but when it comes to Surviving, you've got to think in threes: weaponry, 1v1s, and healing.

So to start, let's take a closer look at understanding the arsenal that will be integral to landing you that Victory Royale. You may be able to build your way out of any threat, but you're going to need to land a shot or two if you want to be the last one standing.

One of the biggest changes introduced in Chapter 2 was a 'reset' of sorts, with a new streamlined arsenal available (I mean, what choice did they have: where do you go from the Boom Bow other than back to square one?). And while the weapons change as often as the Battle Bus departs, with guns coming in, out, and shaken all about (and by shaken all about, we mean vaulted), all you really need to keep track of are the three universal weapon categories: ammo, rarity and type.

WEAPON AMMO

The vast majority of weapons (explosives and melee variations being notable exceptions) in Battle Royale require ammo, but ammo is not a one-size-fits-all situation. Each weapon type has a specific ammo requirement.

Ammo Type	Weapon Type
Light Bullets	Pistols, SMGs
Medium Bullets	Assault Rifles
Heavy Bullets	Sniper Rifles
Shells	Shotguns
Rockets	Rockets - Explosives (Rocket Launchers)

WEAPON RARITY

Weapons fall under the same weapon hierarchy as all items and cosmetics in Fortnite, which indicates both the power of their performance and your chances (be they high or low) of finding them in game.

Common
(★) < Uncommon
(★★) < Rare
(★★★) < Epic
(★★★★) < Legendary
(★★★★★) < Mythic

Chapter 2 introduced Upgrade Benches to the game - this utility allows players to upgrade their weapon's rarity in exchange for materials, eliminating the element of RNG when it comes to weapon power. You can even Sidegrade a weapon for another model of the same rarity, if you want.

Generally speaking, the higher the rarity, the better the weapon - but don't be a slave to the colour system. Don't just mindlessly toss a green weapon in favor of a purple when the green would better serve your current situation. Context is key, and that's where good knowledge of the next category comes into play.

WEAPON TYPE

PISTOLS

Okay, while a Pistol is never anyone's no. 1, it's always a solid option to have in your loadout. These basic guns are effective at close and mid range, and deal decent damage at both. Try using it in a combo with a more range-specific weapon like a Sniper Rifle or SMG.

- Pistols are great fight instigators - use a pistol to close distance before switching to something more powerful up close like a Shotgun or SMG.

- These guns aren't topping any damage charts, so be sure to maximise their efficiency by aiming for the headshot multiplier (2x).

SMGS

SMGs are close range specialists, with a super high fire rate that's balanced by a high damage drop-off and spray. They're easy enough to shoot, so just remember to get up real close before pulling the trigger; SMGs are about as deadly as a breeze from mid to long range.

- SMGs are good tag-team weapons, so use them in tandem with other guns to close the distance before switching to the SMG at close range.

- While the high fire rate means high damage output, it also means it's really easy to lose track of how much ammo you're using. Try to stick to controlled bursts to save bullets.

ASSAULT RIFLES

Assault Rifles are effective across short, mid and long ranges, and their high damage output makes them some of the best weapons in game. They also don't require any cracked FPS mechanics to use: just aim and shoot.

- Assault Rifles have a rough bloom, so shoot in small bursts to keep up the accuracy.

- These guns are hitscan, which require you keep your crosshair on the target and hit them with successive shots.

SNIPER RIFLES

Sniper Rifles are the hardcore cousins of the Assault Rifle. They require top-notch aiming skills to utilise efficiently; they are long range, and rely heavily on a player's tracking ability and the bullet travel speed.

- Sniper Rifles are great for, well, sniping, but they're slow to fire, so be ready to switch to another weapon (short range, preferably) so you're never caught out.

EXPLOSIVES

Sometimes you've got to go in a little more blazing than a mere bullet, and that's where rocket launchers come in. Explosives do a huge amount of damage, but they come at the cost of slow fire and splash damage, so be careful where you're aiming them.

- When it comes to destroying builds, you can't beat explosives. Fire at a build's foundations with a rocket to topple it in no time.

- Remember that it takes time for the rocket to fire and reach its target, so if your target is moving, you'll need to predict their movement and aim ahead accordingly.

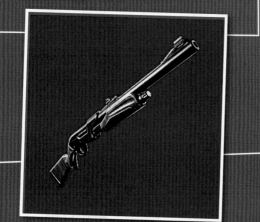

SHOTGUNS

Shotguns are pretty devastating at close range, with a high DPS and area of effect. Unfortunately, the havoc it wreaks at close range comes at the cost of any efficiency from mid to long. They're made to deal big damage up close and personal.

- These guns are made for duelling, so they're best to equip when you're practicing your shoot-build-shoot coordination.

- Keep topping up your ammo - Shotguns are slow to reload, but a partial reload is notably quicker than a full one.

DON'T COUNT 'EM OUT

The Fortnite of yesteryear had quite a colourful arsenal with weapons like Crossbows, and everyone's favourite (sarcasm heavily implied), the Infinity Blade. While they were vaulted with the opening of Chapter 2, the developers have been known to crack open the Vault and put old weapons back into rotation, so don't rule out a comeback in the future. You can always practice with some of the vaulted weapons in Creative mode.

THE 3 BASICS:
SURVIVING - 1V1

There you are, minding your own business and eating an apple in the shade of a tree you're considering hacking down, when a bullet clips your knee out of nowhere and you're thrown in the most frantic, high-tension moment of any Battle Royale: the 1v1 duel.

Of course, there's no way of knowing the skills (or resources) of any of the other 99 players on that island with you, but there's always a good way to prepare yourself for success.

THE LOADOUT

The most important aspect of any 1v1 is what you're working with, and that's all down to your loadout. While everyone has their own unique playstyle and preferences, there's a general balance that you should keep in mind for the most optimal inventory: 2 Weapons - 2 Heals - 1 Bonus.

The weapon slots should prioritise an Assault Rifle over other weaponry, and the Bonus slot is entirely up to you. The 2:2:1 set-up is a good balanced set-up, but it can be customised; if you discover you're a little more aggressively-inclined, maybe a more weapon-heavy set-up is the better fit for you.

SHOOT - BUILD - REPOSITION (REPEAT)

Learn it, live it, breathe it, eat it, repeat it. The Shoot - Build - Reposition mantra is exactly what it says on the tin: pull the trigger, build a quick wall, reposition yourself, and start again. This pattern minimises the amount of damage from incoming fire in a 1v1 by having the wall eat it, while also giving you brief cover time to keep the enemy on their toes by repositioning before continuing the push.

Obviously sometimes you will need to adapt the mantra and build a few times between repositioning, or slide in a few extra shots if your opponent is floundering, but it's a foundational process you need to familiarise yourself with. The more seamless the better, so try practicing in Battle Lab or Creative.

FIND THE HIGH GROUND

Any video game with any kind of gunplay follows the general rule of thumb that High Ground is King; Fortnite is no different. It's always easier to aim/shoot down than up.

While you may find yourself atop a mountain or tower with the ability to spot enemies, you'll more often find yourself having to make your own high ground via your building skills. Be sure to practice the Go-To Builds listed in The 3 Basics: Building section (p. 14-17) to get the high ground advantage before your opponent.

PICK YOUR BATTLES

As silly as it sounds, sometimes the best way to win a 1v1 is knowing when to bow out, or even when not to engage. In a game with countless guns and headshot bonuses, sometimes it's easy to forget the win condition is to be the last one standing, i.e., alive.

If you spot an enemy before they spot you, ask yourself: do you need to take this fight? Do you have the right loadout prepped? Are you in a conducive map environment to engage right now? If the answer is yes, then charge on in; but if not, then you're best sneaking away to heal up, or refill your loadout.

The same thought process should apply mid-fight. If you find yourself against an opponent and you're both building 90s right into the skybox, is it worth burning through all of your resources for this one kill? Unless it's between you and them for Victory Royale, the answer is likely no. Take the fight back down to the ground by taking out their foundations, or even edit yourself a sneaky exit route.

KEEP YOUR MOVEMENT RANDOM

As soon as a duel reaches close range, your survivability relies more heavily on your movement, and the best way to stay alive is to keep it unpredictable. Jumping is an easy way to disorientate the enemy's tracking, and it also gives you a better chance to land a headshot by aiming on your way down.

But you can't just mash jump and hope for the best - the game actually has jump fatigue mechanics, which means every consecutive jump becomes slower and lower. To combat this, you're best to zig-zag between jumping in intervals.

THE 3 BASICS:
SURVIVING - HEALTH AND SHIELDS

The last of the three survival skills to master is a solid knowledge of your health and shields. It's near impossible to pull off a perfect Battle Royale run, but you needn't worry - there's always a second chance (or third, or fourth, or...) if you slip up and get clipped. And with the dawn of Chapter 2 bringing more support options to the table than ever before, there really is no excuse for you to be running around that island at sub-75 HP without a shield or a prayer.

RESTORING HP

Bandages: Bandages are the bread and butter of any support kit, healing 15 HP with a 3 second usage. Unfortunately they have a healing cap of 75 HP, so you'll have to top up by other means if you want to fully restore your Health.

Medkit: The Medkit heals a full 100 HP but comes at the cost of taking a full 10 seconds to use. The only way to use one safely is to ensure you're alone and have good cover before cracking one out. These are far better used post-fight as opposed to mid.

If you're playing in a duo or team, there are multi-target healing items available for you to keep everyone looking green in one move. They make their way in and out of the Vault like clockwork, so keep an eye out for items like the Bandage Bazooka and the Chug Splash coming into rotation if you prefer to play the medic.

RESTORING SHIELDS

The blue bar represents your shield, and protects your HP by absorbing any damage taken until it depletes. Acquiring and topping up your shield should always be pretty close to the top of your priority list once you make your landing, so keep an eye out for the following:

Small Shield Potions: These little guys restore 25 Shield Points, but cannot be used if your shield is already over 50%. They're useful to get started on your shield in early game, and their 2 second usage time makes them a safer option to recharge shields mid-fight.

Shield Potions: A little more heavy duty than the Small iteration, the Shield Potion restores 50 Shield Points. They take 5 seconds to use, but can fully restore your Shields if double stacked.

It can be hard to balance Health/Shield item usage in-game, but you should always try to prioritize using smaller items. Why? Well, they may be less effective overall, but they're quick to use and can give you the small burst of energy you need before returning to action. Heavier duty items are always going to be the riskier option.

FORAGED FOODS

Foraged foods are different from regular items as they can be consumed directly from picking them up from the ground (handy, since the majority only take 1 second to gobble down). You can find them scattered across the island in a variety of locations, and provide an array of small, yet notable, health-related benefits.

Apples: The teacher's favourite grants 5 HP, and they tend to spawn in clusters near trees, like in the Orchard.

Corn: And corn is the last of the 5 HP-granting foraged foods. These can be found by destroying crops in Frenzy Farm.

Mushrooms: Mushrooms are a little more valuable than the average foraged food as they grant 5 Shield Points when eaten - oh, and there's no cap, so you can chomp your way to a full shield, if you find enough. They usually grow in swampy areas.

Slurpshrooms: The Slurpshroom is the evolved mushroom, with the ability to heal 10 HP or Shield Points over 2 seconds. Like Mushrooms, they can be found in swampy areas.

Bananas: Like the apple, bananas grant 5 HP when eaten. They can generally be found on the ground of more tropical biomes.

Cabbages: Cabbages are the beefier (so to speak) HP restoration food, granting 10 HP when eaten. They can be found in farmland locations, like the Orchard or Frenzy Farm.

Coconuts: Coconuts grant 5 HP (or regen shield if the player's HP is already full). These can generally be found on the ground near palm trees.

Peppers: Peppers are unique because they're the only foraged food to provide something other than just Health/Shields. Eating a pepper grants 5 HP and a 20% boost to your movement speed for 60 seconds.

TIP:

The ultimate foraged item is the fabled Golden Mushroom, a rare item introduced in Chapter 2, Season 3. It grants 100 Shield Points when eaten, but it's nigh impossible to find - with data miners suggesting it has a 0.0001% chance to spawn.

||||:

Health and Shield items were not immune from the grand culling of Chapter 2; plenty of hallmark staples like the Cozy Campfire and the OG Chug Jug were Vaulted on the other side of the black hole. But hey, you know by now that nothing in the Vault is necessarily there forever, so keep an eye out online for patch notes when a new update lands to see what restorative items are in play.

GONE FISHIN'

Thanks to the new fishing mechanic, there's a whole new gamut of guppies that can top up your HP. These fish are actually super valuable when it comes to healing, as all three types are more efficient in healing than their item equivalent - i.e., Small Fry are more valuable than Bandages, Floppers are more valuable than Medkits, and Slurpfish are more valuable than Shield Potions.

Their biggest benefit is that fish only take 1 second to consume, which is on par with foraged foods as being the quickest consumables in-game, but with a way bigger health restoration on offer. Check out the Fishing for a Win chapter p. 28-29 for more information on fish and their healing properties.

FISHING FOR A WIN

One of the biggest changes that Chapter 2 brought to the island was the fishing system: a tried-and-true relaxation mechanic found in MMOs from the dawn of time, now with an added pinch of battle royale panic and a promise of loot, health bonuses, and insta-kill projectile goldfish. Yeah, you read that right: insta-kill projectile goldfish.

But fishing isn't just a great excuse to kick back and drag up some rare weapons from the fathoms below. It's also a great way to make progress in your season tiers and earn progression medals to earn new rare Battle Pass skins.

FISHING 101

First and foremost, you've got to find the perfect spot. You can fish in either active locations (look out for the telltale white circle of water and fish below) or in calm waters. If you can pick, prioritize active locations: you'll get better rewards.

Next, you need to swap your handgun for something more harmonious: a fishing rod. Rods take up a slot in your inventory, so to use one, simply select it, aim at some water and press and hold your fire button. When you've chosen where to place your bobber according to the range meter, release fire and cast a line!

Then comes the wait. Chill out (but stay vigilant - this is still a battle royale, remember!) until your bobber dips under the surface, and then hit fire once more to reel in your catch. Be quick! If you're sleeping on the fire button when your catch bites, it'll swim away.

FINDING A ROD

Fishing rods spawn all across the map in barrels (and sometimes in treasure chests). If you're looking to fish, head down to a dock or anywhere that looks like a prime angling spot and you'll likely find a rod barrel ready for use.

CATCH OF THE DAY

So what lies beneath? Other than a variety of weapons and building materials, there are a bunch of (surprise, surprise) fish up for grabs that have various boons and bonuses ready to bestow upon its catcher. Here are the three you're most likely to come across:

Fish	Rarity	Carry Limit	Effect
Smallfry	Common	6	Heals 25 HP (up to 75%)
Flopper	Uncommon	4	Heals 50 HP
Slurpfish	Epic	3	Heals 50 HP/Shield

You can also haul up some Rusty Cans, which may look like, well, utter garbage, but can pull through in a weapon-dry pinch as they can deal 20 damage. Of course, if luck is truly on your side, then you may also come across the fabled Mythic Goldfish.

THE MYTHIC GOLDFISH

So let's address the elephant in the room: despite the fact it's called a 'Goldfish', it's technically a Goldfish trophy. Hurling this hunk of freshwater flounder at an opponent will land a whopping 200 damage, dealing a one-shot kill and endless shame to the downed enemy.

However, the 'Mythic' part of the name is pretty accurate. This item has a 1 in a million chance of appearing, and when we say 1 in a million, we don't mean "oh, yeah, like it's very rare"; we're talking stats. During the Fortnite Fishing Frenzy event held in November 2019, over 25 million fish were caught, but only 34 Bottom Feeder pickaxes (the grand prize for landing a Mythic Goldfish) were awarded. 34. Out of over 25,000,000. Which comes to about... a 0.000136% chance.

PICK YOUR PLAYSTYLE

Since 2017, Fortnite's gameplay has continually evolved (and sometimes deliberately devolved when the devs recognised they got a little too spicy the previous season), with new elements and mechanics introduced that have drawn the game further and further from a simple aim-and-shoot Battle Royale.

While Fortnite doesn't employ the same class system as a lot of its genre-competitors, the game is definitely enabled to allow the player to take on a distinct playstyle depending on their own gameplay preferences. Whether you prefer to cinch that victory with a point blank headshot at close range or a sneaky snipe from a bush, there's room for you in Fortnite, and a Victory Royale waiting for you and your playstyle.

THE CLASSIC

The Classic playstyle is when a player uses a little bit of all of the game's mechanics to earn a Victory Royale instead of specializing or focusing on one or two. A Jack of All Trades, if you will. This is the standard Fortnite experience, with players working with a balanced loadout, outrunning the storm, engaging in a little gunplay, a little building, a little looting here and there.

This playstyle is best for those who want a more casual experience when playing, as it is accessible and well-suited to all skill levels. As the name implies, it's a timeless playstyle that will always work in every Season, and regularly has new elements thrown in to spice things up every now and then.

THE HUNTER

If you're coming into Fortnite from more FPS-heavy games, then you may be more inclined to the Hunter playstyle. The Hunter drops into the island with the objective to take you out, and if all goes to plan, you won't even see it coming. Hunters take full advantage of stealth options available, almost always have the natural high ground advantage and are masters of the long range snipe to take out unsuspecting opponents.

The Hunter playstyle has an extremely high skill-ceiling and is definitely best suited to those who have honed their aiming skills. This is a style that requires familiarity with the map, the arsenal and weapon combos, and is most efficient for those with some experience under their belts.

THE MEDIC

This playstyle is duo/team-exclusive, and while it has been viable since the game's launch, the new additions to Chapter 2 really helped facilitate those who prefer to leave the conflict to their teammates and play more of a supportive role from a safer distance. Chapter 2 allows you to heal your squad from afar with items like the Bandage Bazooka and the Chug Splash, and carry your downed teammates to safety. The Medic's loadout is always going to be more healing based than aggressive, and is always well equipped to make a quick exit if a teamfight goes awry.

The Medic style is better suited for those who enjoy playing with others, and don't necessarily revel in lining up headshots or jumping in the frenzied panic of a shotgun 1v1. This allows you to still be a vital part of the action but in a more support-strategic sense.

THE ARCHITECT

Fortnite is unique in its building mechanics, and while you can get by with some basic 1x1s, some players prefer to delve deeper into the world of construction possibilities. Architects can stack 90s until the cows come home and will rely on building the battle into the skies should they be forced to duel. Be wary of entering an Architect's build to take them on - they love a good trap, and are also well-versed in making speedy edits to take the ground out from beneath your feet.

This playstyle is perhaps the hardest to master as it requires borderline muscle-memory key inputs to pull off at top levels. Architects hone their skills in Creative and the Battle Lab, continuously working on faster ways to throw up their defenses.

PRO SURVIVAL TIPS

With all of the knowledge bestowed upon you in the previous 30 pages or so, you're almost ready to take on the island and claim that Victory Royale. Almost.

So before you take that big leap off the Battle Bus, take a moment to browse over these last minute (yet no less important) survival tips to take out your opponents, clear out the island and take home the metaphorical trophy.

PLAY AROUND THE STORM

- Never forget about the storm! So much of your obstacles are PVP based that it's easy to forget about the environmental element that can take you out in a heartbeat. You can't defeat the storm, so be smart and play around it.

- When the storm shrinks, try to stay around its edges. Players tend to move as far into the middle of the Eye as they can; the fringes are always less busy.

- Hanging around the edges is also a good strategy when the Eye is shrinking. When you're in the clear, take cover and snipe out any approaching players running into safety.

- Remember that the storm does more damage during later stages of the game, so it gets more and more dangerous to find yourself stuck in as the game goes on.

- Make sure to close doors behind you. It will cover your tracks and also alert you if any player enters the structure after you.

- Before entering a building, look out for signs of another player having been there. Other than open doors, opened treasure chests and broken walls are surefire signs that someone else is around. Of course, there's a chance that they're long gone, but it's always better to be safe than sorry.

LOOT LIFE

- Instinct tells you to loot the opponent you just picked off, but you're always best waiting. There's a good chance your fight has drawn some attention, so be sure to scout the area for others before letting your defences down and pilfering through your enemy's belongings.

- If you do suspect that someone is nearby, you can also use your enemy's loot as bait. Leave the items out and take cover before sniping the unsuspecting player you lured in. But remember, it works both ways! So don't just go running up to abandoned piles of loot on the ground without a second thought.

LISTEN UP

KEEP CAUTIOUS

- Make good use of the third-person camera by using it as peripheral vision. You can position your character at a wall and use the camera to check for enemies around the corner while safely in cover.

- Never fully take down a tree when harvesting - they have a distinct disappearance animation that could catch an enemy's attention, even from afar.

- Sound plays as much of a key role in survival as sight. If possible, play with headphones instead of speakers. You'll be able to pick up a lot more audio details you may have otherwise missed.

- Always listen out for footsteps when out in the open or looting a building - it's the telltale sign that another player is nearby. It's unlikely you'll be able to pin the exact location of the enemy but it should allow you to prepare for a pending offence.

- Be cautious of the noise that you're making, too. If you're trying to stay on the DL, opt for walking and crouching for a quieter mode of movement. You can toggle default running in the settings.

- Try to save switching and reloading weapons for when you're alone. Switching/reloading prompts an audio cue, and there are actually different sounds for each weapon type, which could give a nearby enemy a tip as to what you're rolling with.

WELCOME TO THE ISLAND

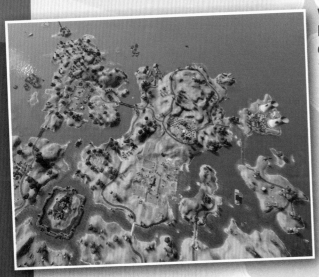

When Fortnite launched back in 2017, players were dropped onto one island that they slowly grew to know, learn, write several in-depth guides for and maybe even love, slightly, across a span of seasons over two years. It was familiar. It was home.

And then Chapter 2 came in like a wrecking ball, wiping the map we knew and loved (and most importantly, it bears repeating: knew) from the face of the digital earth and replacing it with a new island for players to explore and get to know all over again. While there were anchors of familiarity here and there with carry-over locations (like trusty old Pleasant Park), Chapter 2's map is, for the most part, new territory to explore for gamers new and old alike.

OUT IN THE OPEN

This map is definitely less crowded than the previous iteration. There are less large structures, which lends itself to the more open gameplay vibes from the early days of Fortnite.

THE BIG BLUE

Hope you're ready to get wet, because this map's major new feature is big, blue and a touch moist. This island has a lot of water, adding a whole new bunch of elements to the gameplay loop. Water plays a huge part in how you can get around the island in Chapter 2.

A TRICK OF THE EYE

The map may feel bigger because it's way more open, but it's actually a touch smaller than the old island. Interestingly, while the new map clocks in more square footage than the old one, the amount of playable space means the first map was actually about 2-3% bigger.

HERE THIS SEASON, GONE THE NEXT

While the parameters stay the same, the island itself is ever-changing. Chapter 2 - Season 3 saw a mammoth revamp by flooding the map, covering most of the lands players had worked so hard to get to know with huge bodies of water. What's next? An earthquake? Avalanche? Black hole? Hey, never say never.

WAS THAT ALWAYS THERE?

Yes, your focus may be on the other 99 players on the island, but also keep an eye out for anything peculiar or out of the ordinary on the map as you play. Epic is known for teasing new features and updates with hints across the map - and sometimes even in spawn.

STICKING THE LANDING

The name of the game in Battle Royale is survival, and it doesn't begin with a gunshot - it begins as soon as you leap out of that Battle Bus, and where you end up landing pretty much dictates where you end up placing in the grand scheme of things.

This is a race to be the last one standing, and like any good race, you've got to be quick off of the blocks. You've got to touch ground fast, but you've also got to combine that with precision. It's about choosing the best landing spot and getting there ASAP.

A LEAP OF FAITH

It all begins when you leap from the Battle Bus, and that's where your brain better start whirling into action. Read up on these tips in advance and keep them in mind when you make your next jump:

WHERE TO LAND

1. Know your Hot Drops. A Hot Drop is an area that's a popular pick for players to land. These areas tend to be among the direct Battle Bus trajectory, or are known to be particularly loot-heavy. There tend to be a lot of early skirmishes here, so they're best to be avoided if you want to focus on building your loadout when you land instead of dodging headshots.

2. But hey, if you do find yourself heading for a Hot Drop because a challenge dictates it (or you're just a blood-thirsty wildling like that), then keep an exit strategy in mind as you begin your descent. It could be as simple as spotting a boat on your way down, just remember: get in, get what you need, get out.

3. Look out for other players. The majority of a match's eliminations occur during the landing when everyone's still clearing out their zone, so aim for a more sparsely populated spot, if you can. Try to get some distance from the Battle Bus route if you're going Solo, but you can afford to go more central if you're in a team (there's safety in numbers, after all).

HOW TO LAND

TIP

Remember when choosing a spot, don't go too remote. Landing is a balance between safety and resources. There may be the odd weapon or bandage nearby that lone shack you chose to hit up, but you'll be spending a lot more time trying to scrape together your loadout than you will if you take the risk and land in the larger, named locations.

2. Okay, but once you go low, you've then gotta aim high (I know, stay with me here). The glider deployment is unavoidable, so as soon as that sucker pops out, you've got to start looking for some verticality in the vicinity. Always land on a roof rather than the middle of a street - it gives you high-ground advantage over other players in the area, and easy access to harvestable materials and hidden chests tucked away in structures.

TIP

Landing Tip #2: After deploying your glider, aim the camera at the ground and press forward to hit the ground faster.

TIP

Don't save any Shields if you find them early on. Glug 'em down ASAP.

AND WE'RE OFF!

You better be ready to take off as soon as you land, because Battle Royale is not a game for dawdling - you'll have to save your congratulatory self high-five for nailing the perfect landing later. Your loadout needs attending to.

1. The first rule is to go low. Your descent has two stages: skydive and glide. Your glider will auto-deploy when your character is a certain distance from the ground, which means it'll pop out a lot sooner if you're over a mountain than say, a road or a ravine. The downside to this is that skydiving is way faster, so you want to aim for lower ground to maximise your dive time and landing speed.

Prioritise finding a close-range weapon (shotguns are ideal) to defend yourself should you come across another player while configuring your loadout. Harvest everything in sight so you've got a decent base to begin with, and once you've found some form of mid-long range weapon and some healing, you're ready to take off and take out anyone that gets in your way.

GETTING AROUND THE MAP

Once you've leaped off of the Battle Bus to your prime landing spot, it's time to start your shooting and looting journey all across the island - and you don't have to do it all on foot.

Fortnite has always had a myriad of interesting ways for you to make your way across the map (we're talking from floating red balloons and pirate cannons to portable rifts and killer mech suits), but like with most gameplay aspects, the devs decided to wipe the slate clean with Chapter 2 and start over. While the Great Mobility Cull of Chapter 2 saw it launch with only one vehicle, the list of mobility options available ingame has continued to grow with each new update.

MOTORBOAT

- Seats: 4
- HP: 800

When Chapter 2 launched, the Motorboat was the one and only vehicle available for players to use to charter the new map (makes sense, with the new focus on bodies of water and all). While the vehicular options have expanded since then, the Motorboat is still the main method of travel across the island, with over 50 spawn locations over the map.

Each Motorboat can carry up to a squad of four, and comes equipped with a boost for extra speed and a single-shot rocket launcher that can deal 35 damage. You can also drive/boost your boat into players to launch them and inflict fall damage.

TIP:
You can even drive your Motorboat across land, but know that it depletes 1 HP per second, and also makes a hell of a lot of noise while doing so. You won't be able to sneak up on anyone in one of these.

CHOPPA

- Seats: 5
- HP: 1500

The CHOPPA arrived in Patch 12.20 and let players take their vendettas to the skies. While it doesn't come with any weaponry included, it's a juggernaut in its own right, with 1500 HP and the ability to crash into and destroy buildings.

While the CHOPPA may have a more robust HP, it actually has several weak points. Shooting the rotors (including the tail rotors) deals x2.25 damage to the vehicle. Players can also shoot out the glass windshield. It can also be used as an explosive device when its HP reaches 0, as the resulting explosion deals 70 damage to players and 450 to buildings.

TIP:

Keep in mind that jumping from the CHOPPA won't redeploy your glider, so be prepared to break your fall before you leap unless you want to deal with fall damage. If you don't have a Crash Pad or mats to build, aim for water.

ZIPLINE

Ziplines made their debut back in OG Season 7, giving your mobility a quick boost from Point A to B while still allowing you the ability to use your weapons and items. Ziplines are also a great way to scope out the area and spot enemies.

Of course, the danger of becoming a zipping duck is very real with ziplines, so if an enemy spots you mid-zip, be prepared to drop off at a random point to disrupt your predicted trajectory and throw them off. Ziplines have no capacity limit, so the same goes if you start zipping with an unexpected plus one. There's no fall damage to worry about when it comes to ziplines, so don't be afraid to drop it like it's hot if you find yourself with company.

TIP:
If you have to draw a weapon while zipping, go for hitscan - they're a lot easier to use while moving.

LAUNCH PAD/ GLIDER

Throw down a Launch Pad to throw yourself up into the air and take to the skies. The pad is ideal to gain some quick verticality without having to scale any mountains, redeploy your Glider and sail out of harm's way.

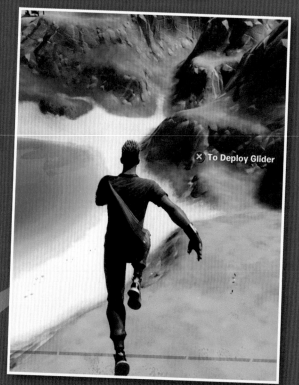

The Launch Pad/Glider combo can be your best friend if you find yourself stuck in the dreaded storm - it's a much faster way to get yourself back into the eye than on foot. It can also be used offensively, to launch players into roof traps.

I'LL TAKE IT TO-GO

While the mobility options may be pared back, this is still Fortnite - the game with Meowscles' Peow Peow Rifle. Of course there are other... uh, unorthodox ways to travel around the island. Whether it be wrangling yourself a Loot Shark for a quick zip across the water, wielding Jules' Glider Gun or launching yourself from a Pirate Cannon, there will always be alternative methods of transport available. Keep an eye out for the patch notes each update to find out the new ways to make your way around the island.

TIP:

A Launch Pad has infinite uses, but be careful - it can be used by anyone on the map. That may mean the very enemy you were trying to escape can jump right on and glide down after you, so don't let your guard down just because you're in.

MAKING PROGRESS

TRACK PROGRESS & EARN XP!

- Experiment on the island to **DISCOVER PUNCH CARDS.**
- **REACH MILESTONES** in each punch card to **EARN XP.**

I CALL SHOTGUN

...BLE-DIPPING

⊗ **GOT IT!**

Perhaps one of Fortnite's biggest strengths is the endless gameplay loop - there's no 'end' in sight when it comes to dropping into the island, wiping out everyone there, queuing up and going again. But there's something in the basic human condition that craves a good progression system, which Epic delivered to those with a bit of drive and flair for the creative in two forms: XP and V-Bucks.

XP

XP (Experience Points) is a progression system in Fortnite that allows a player to level up. Since there are no stats in Fortnite, leveling up is pertinent to gaining access to in-game content, like progressing through the Battle Pass to unlock cosmetics. You can earn XP just by playing the game itself, but you can also earn bonuses depending on your match performance.

There are three types of XP: Survival, Combat and Match. Each category has its own sub-variants and whatnot but it's a pretty basic system: the longer you survive and the more kills you rack up, the more XP you're rewarded.

TIPS TO BOOST YOUR XP GAIN:

• **Get Ready to Rumble:**

Playing Team Rumble lets you chain together a bunch of eliminations and assists, as well as a maximum possible survival reward guaranteed.

TIP:

Keep an eye out for XP coins while you're playing - they don't require any actions to acquire and snagging one will net you easy XP.

- **Keep Up Your APM:**

Don't let your thumbs fall idle when you're playing; you can earn XP from loads of basic in-game actions from fishing and upgrading to searching ammo boxes and chests. Keep busy to keep your XP uptick going.

- **Lay Low:**

The longer you play, the less opportunities there are to find unopened chests and get their XP. Try to land in low-key areas away from the horde - that way you get first dibs on the XP in the area without worrying about getting eliminated straight off the bat.

TIP:

Warning! Never click on any links online that promise free V-bucks. Countless scam sites try to prey on desperate gamers looking for a quick boost to buy a new cosmetic – these are all fake, and may result in your account being stolen, as well as your personal information. That hamburger head isn't worth your identity. Stay vigilant.

V-BUCKS

Of course, the other way to get access to cosmetics is to use V-Bucks, Fortnite's in-game currency that you can drop at the Item Shop so you can finally get that ribbon dancer emote you've been dreaming of.

V-Bucks can be bought with real-world currency, but hold on — you don't have to crack open your wallet just yet, as there are plenty of ways in-game to earn the V-Bucks you need to get the cosmetic you so desire.

THE BATTLE PASS

The fabled Battle Pass is another in-game progression system that rewards players for the completion of gameplay challenges. There's a Free Pass, but it has a limited amount of tasks compared to the full pass. The full Battle Pass costs V-Bucks to acquire, but hey - you've gotta spend money to make money, and the Battle Pass more than returns its initial investment if you make your way through it.

TIP:

Remember! You can actually make enough V-Bucks with the free challenges to purchase a full Battle Pass. A little grinding never hurt anyone.

The Battle Pass challenges have a wide range of asks, from visiting certain landmarks and kicking soccer balls to eliminating x-amount of opponents and surviving specific falls. Completing the challenges keeps the Battle Royale gig relatively fresh with new objectives other than the usual beat-the-storm-and-everyone-in-it shtick. And doing so will level up your pass, enabling you to hit those V-Buck reward milestones (15 times, if you're lucky. That's up to 1,500 V-Bucks, if quick maths isn't your thing).

HOW LONG WILL YOU SURVIVE?

You've gotten this far, so there's a reasonable assumption to make that you've actually read the last 43 pages or so. We've imparted all of the wisdom we have upon you, and you should be ready to leap out of that Battle Bus and unleash a calculating bloodthirst of chaos onto all of those unsuspecting fools down below. But how much did you really retain? Time to put your knowledge to the test and see how long you'd survive on the island...

2. **Which structure has the highest maximum HP?**

a. Metal wall

b. Stone ramp

c. Metal roof

d. Wooden wall

1. **What's the ideal balance for a loadout?**

a. 1 Weapon: 1 Heal: 3 Bonus

b. 2 Weapons: 2 Heals: 1 Bonus

c. 1 Weapon: 3 Heals: 1 Bonus

d. 4 Weapon: 0 Heal: 1 Bonus

3. **What is the most time/ recovery efficient form of healing?**

a. Medkit

b. Chug Jug

c. Apple

d. Fish

4. Where is the best place to shoot to take down a CHOPPA?

a. Tail tractor

b. Wing

c. Tractors

d. Windshield

8. What would be the best combo to close distance?

a. Sniper rifle, SMG

b. Pistol, shotgun

c. Assault rifle, shotgun

d. Pistol, SMG

5. What is the 1v1 mantra?

a. Shoot - Build - Reposition

b. Build - Shoot - Reposition

c. Shoot - Build - Reload

d. Build - Shoot - Reload

9. What is the strongest defensive build?

a. Turtle

b. 1x1

c. Reinforced Ramp

d. Basic Ramp

6. What is the best build move to escape a duel?

a. Build a reinforced ramp

b. Build a basic ramp

c. Build and edit in an back exit

d. Build up with 90s

10. What's the general rule for the quickest landing?

a. Aim high, go low.

b. Aim low, go high.

c. Go low, aim high.

d. Go high, aim low.

7. What is the best healing item you can fish?

a. Rusty Can

b. Slurpfish

c. Smallfry

d. Flopper

11. Which weapon type is best when mobile?

a. Throwable

b. Projectile

c. Hitscan

d. Melee

Answers P62

A FRIEND LIKE FORTNITE

Over the years, Fortnite has certainly racked up an impressive (and eclectic) list of collaborators; from the Avengers and Michael Jordan to John Wick and Godzilla, there's no entity too out there to fit into the wonderful world of Fortnite. And 2020 was no exception; with the addition of Party Royale and the continued expansion of crossovers on the main island, the year saw some of the highest-profile names added to Fortnite's roster yet. Did you manage to catch any of these limited time collabs?

FORTNITE X NFL

It's not a countdown to Superbowl Sunday without all 32 NFL team skins being available to don in Battle Royale. January saw the return of the popular NFL-related content, this time with a new on-stream tournament for players to watch and cheer for as Fortnite pros paired with some of the NFL's best players to represent their team in the Streamer Bowl.

FORTNITE X AQUAMAN

It was only a matter of time before DC's Aquaman floated into Fortnite, and what better time than the grand flood of Chapter 2 - Season 3? June 2020 saw the King of the Ocean make his way to join the rest of the Justice League on the water-logged island, in both his fully-suited golden armor and shirtless Jason Momoa glory variations.

FORTNITE X DEADPOOL

Marvel's Deadpool made his Fortnite debut in Chapter 2 - Season 2 back in April, but he didn't come alone: the motor-mouthed merc brought along his friends Cable, Psylocke and Domino in the subsequent X-Force expansion. In true Deadpool fashion, it wasn't enough to just to drop in with some skins, but also a slew of uniquely Wade Wilson-esque Challenges ranging from finding his secret hideout to not saying thank you to the drop bus driver.

FORTNITE X TRAVIS SCOTT

Rap star Travis Scott made his mark on Fortnite with the Astronomical event, but his digital footprint on the island went beyond the world premiere of his new track. The rapper was added to the Icon Series, with Outfits, Emotes and exclusive-themed items like the Astroworld Cyclone Glider and even Travis-based loading screens added to the game.

FORTNITE X HARLEY QUINN

2020 was a big year for DC's Harley Quinn as she went solo from the Suicide Squad both in the movie-verse and world of Fortnite in February. The Harley Quinn bundle launched in the Item Shop with new outfits and weapons, with Challenges available to suit up with her Always Fantabulous Harley look instead of the classic Lil Monster XoXo Harley.

FORTNITE X STAR WARS

Star Wars dipped its first toe in the Fortnite pool at the end of 2019, but made a triumphant return to celebrate May 4th (Star Wars day, if you didn't know). Players could add a galactic flair to their arsenal and wardrobe with a variety of exclusive lightsaber weapons and Star Wars inspired skins and outfits, including Rey, Kylo Ren and the classic Trooper.

PRACTICE MAKES PERFECT: CREATIVE + BATTLE LAB

When it comes to Fortnite, there's no truer idiom than the old classic: practice makes perfect. Sure, you can memorize weapon stats and healing efficiencies until you're blue in the face, but it's not until you actively put them to use that you can really learn. But the Battle Royale island isn't the best place to practice your 90s when there are 99 other players out there trying to put a bullet in your brain...

That's where Creative and Battle Lab come into play - places for you to practice and perfect your craft without the pressure of imminent assassination.

CREATIVE

Creative has been in play for a while now - it's the self-explanatory mode that allows players to create, build and share their own islands via the Creative hub world.

My Island: The power of creativity comes from your AR phone, a smart device that can levitate a treasure chest or duplicate a million housebarns. It can be a daunting beginning your masterpiece from literal nothingness, so you can start with some ready-made prefabs (pre-built structures and existing Fortnite assets).

Featured Islands: If you want to try something different, then Featured Islands are perfect for you. These have been created by other users and hand-picked by Epic as some of the best the community has to offer. You can find the current picks in the Creative Hub, and you can enter them via rifts.

Oh, and if you want to see your own creation featured, you can submit your island to the official Epic Games site. You can also find tips there as to what the developers are looking for when it comes to reviewing submissions.

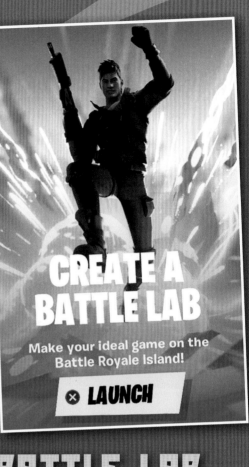

CREATE A BATTLE LAB

Make your ideal game on the Battle Royale Island!

⊗ **LAUNCH**

TIP:

If you're looking for something in particular, you can access other islands created by users via the Island Codes system. Island Codes are 12-digit strings unique to each island, and they can be input into the hub world rifts. You can find a bunch of Island Codes online - just Google.

TIP:

Enemy Bots are great for practicing various combat situations without having to take part in an actual match. This can be a great way to build up your combat skills outside of the arena if you prefer some private practice. Bots obviously can't replicate the playstyle of a human opponent, but they're definitely useful to familiarize yourself with using weapons, combos, and running drills.

BATTLE LAB

Battle Lab was a Chapter 2 addition, and is the better option for those who want to create their own game mode instead of their own game arena. Battle Lab uses the standard Battle Royale island but lets you call the shots when it comes to game rules. In layman's terms: it's Creative mode without any of the building.

Create Your Own LTM: Battle Lab allows you to create your own Battle Royale mode. Like Creative, it can be a little intimidating starting from scratch, so Epic allows you access to existing LTM rules as a starting point if you'd prefer. You can decide on a bunch of parameters (from loot drops to the effects of gravity) and when you're done with your settings, you can fill the game with up to 15 friends and start the chaos.

Bot Grenades: Bot Grenades are unique items to Battle Lab that allow for custom combat scenarios. These Grenades come in two variations - Friendly and Enemy - and create AI-controlled characters to spawn where the item is thrown.

PARTY ROYALE

PARTY ROYALE

EARLY ACCESS

All Chill, No Sweat
Leave your weapons and mats behind.

Hang Out With Friends
Race around obstacle courses by land or sea, perfect your skydive, go fishing with friends, and more.

The Party's Just Getting Started
Stay tuned for updates soon!

LOADING

You can use the Ping button to mark locations and items to alert squadmates.

This experimental space is unique from other Fortnite modes in two major ways: no crafting, no weapons. Party Royale participants can chill out, listen to music, and compete in a variety of challenges solo or with friends - all on a brand new, exclusive island map. Sometimes it's just nice to put down the rocket launcher and enjoy some chill time without the worry of imminent assassination, you know?

MAKE MESS, NOT WAR

This island may be a no-death zone but it wouldn't be Fortnite without the ability to wield some sort of target-based machinery. You may not be able to cause a massacre with these Party Royale weapons, but you can certainly make a mess.

Paint Wars: Pick a side and start a paintball fight with the purple and orange variants of the Paint Launchers and Paint Grenades.

Food Fight: Hurl a Burger or Tomato at a player to live out your school cafeteria fantasy but with significantly less consequences.

Plumber's Revenge: Take aim with a Plunger Bow, because... Well, why not, really? Why not.

TIP:
You can pick up these non-lethal weapons in vending machines and by fishing.

EXCLUSIVE EMOTES

Since Party Royale has a more social focus, it makes sense that it comes with its own set of emotes to make communicating with your friends while you hang out that much easier. These emotes are exclusive to Party Royale mode, so be sure to check them out while you have them!

WELCOME TO THE PARTY

One of the major things Party Royale brings to the table is a brand new map for players to explore. It may be smaller than the Battle Royale island, but what it lacks in size it certainly makes up for in offerings; whether you're looking to hula dance to Travis Scott in the concert hall, take part in a skydiving time trial or even do sweet nothing, the island has a space for you.

PLACES OF INTEREST

- Main Stage
- The Big Screen
- Skydive Rift
- The Plaza
- Fishstick's Boat Race

THINGS TO DO:

- Quadcrasher racing
- Soccer
- Skydiving
- Aerial obstacle course

DIPLO PRESENTS: THOMAS WESLEY

Watch the Diplo Presents: Thomas Wesley premiere featuring special guests Young Thug and Noah Cyrus live at the Main Stage on June 25 at 9:00 PM ET!

CLOSE

PARTY ROYALE EVENTS

Party Royale brought a whole other world to explore and experience in Fortnite when it landed, but it also literally brought a whole other world to the game: reality. 2020 saw a string of headlining events from the real world to the Party Royale digital realm, how many did you manage to make it to?

PARTY ROYALE PREMIERE

Party Royale launched May 2020 with a bang - a huge concert event opening party with Steve Aoki, deadmau5 and Dillon Francis headlining back-to-back sets at the island's Main Stage.

PARTY FAVOURS:

Did you make it to the party on time? Players who logged in to the Party Royale premiere were given music-reactive Neon Wings Back Bling in commemoration of the event.

ASTRONOMICAL

While the DJ event was the official launch of Party Royale, it's fair to say the concept itself really kicked off back with Travis Scott's Astronomical event in April. Over 27.7 million unique viewers caught the concert and world debut of the new Travis Scott track, showcasing the endless opportunities of the new event-based experiences that Fortnite could provide beyond Battle Royale.

MOVIE NIGHT

In a totally unprecedented (and quite honestly, totally unexpected) move, movie director Christopher Nolan chose the island to debut a trailer for his 2020 sci-fi thriller, Tenet. The Big Screen outdoor theater debuted the trailer on May 21st, with hourly replays.

And following the trailer debut, Epic went on to show three of Nolan's quintessential full-length films on the Big Screen. It was the first test run of Movie Nite, with Inception, Batman Begins and the Prestige available depending on region.

RECORD BREAKERS

As one of the biggest games in the world, it should come as no surprise that Fortnite has managed to rack up more than its fair share of records in the gaming industry. And while they already had some impressive numbers under their belt, the dawn of Chapter 2 brought Epic even more accolades and bragging rights.

ASTRONOMICAL ATTENDEES

Travis Scott took to Fortnite for his first virtual performance and not only was it Astronomical in name, but also in numbers. The concert brought 12.3 million concurrent players, a record-breaking number across the Battle Royale genre. Luckily the previous record holder wasn't too upset about the news about being usurped - Epic previously held it with 10.9 million players during 2019's Marshmello concert.

2019: ONE FOR THE HISTORY BOOKS

Fortnite may be popular but it has the numbers to back itself up, with 2019 grossing $1.8 billion in sales, the highest figure for any single-year sales total in videogame history. It's even more impressive when you factor in that Fortnite is, at its core, a free-to-play model, and continues to thrive simply by offering cosmetic items.

DOOMSDAY DRAWS

There's nothing quite like the end of days to draw a crowd, and Fortnite certainly discovered the fact as its Chapter 2 - Season 2 Doomsday event 'The Device' brought in a total of 2.3 million viewers on Twitch across a variety of channels. This shattered the previous 1.7 million viewer record set by the League of Legends World Championships. It was a sweet revenge of sorts for Fortnite, as the League of Legends record had just edged out Fortnite's own Black Hole event record of 1.7 million viewers by a smidge to snatch the title.

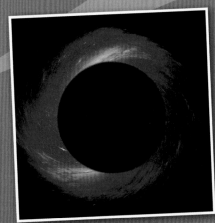

ANYWHERE, EVERYWHERE

With the next-gen announcement in Summer 2020, Fortnite is now available on nine - yes, count them, nine - different gaming platforms: Windows, macOS, Nintendo Switch, PlayStation 4, PlayStation 5, Xbox One, Xbox Series X, iOS and Android. Now there's no excuse to not play - it's truly inescapable.

ESPORTS INVESTMENT

2020 may have been a tricky year for Epic's Esports efforts, but Fortnite still reigns supreme as the largest Esport in the world by monetary prize value. Epic invested a record-breaking $100 million dollars into its Esports scene, breaking the reward for the most money awarded in a year for a single game title.

FORTNITE COMPETITIVE 2020

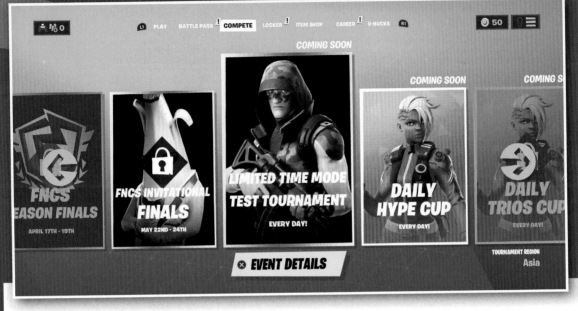

2020 came with its... fair share of obstacles,and unfortunately, even the virtual world of Fortnite was affected, as Epic Games was forced to press pause on their ever-accelerating competitive scene and cancel the Fortnite World Cup 2020 after a record-breaking 2019.

Still, Fortnite may have been down, but it certainly wasn't out; Epic knew the best way to deliver bad news is with a consolation prize, and boy, did they come prepared. World Cup glory may be off the cards, but there's still plenty to play for over in the Arena. Online is the new offline.

DID YOU KNOW?

The 2019 Fortnite World Cup was one of the biggest gaming events of all time. It drew in 2.3 million viewers online and had 19,000 in attendance over the three-day event.

GET HYPE!

Hype isn't just the vibe du jour when playing competitive; it's also the currency, dictating your eligibility to enter certain tournaments or contests. Hype points can be earned in the Arena mode based on both your placement in a match and the amount of eliminations you rack up. Your Hype points dictate which Division you're placed in. Everyone starts in Open League, Division One, but can rank all the way up to Division 10: Champion Division III if you earn enough Hype Points.

WANT TO PARTICIPATE? TRY FORTNITE HYPE NITE

Hype Nite is the most accessible of Fortnite's competitive offerings, geared towards lower-level players with a 1,500 maximum Hype requirement for entry. This your pass to the Championships, essentially. Everyone's gotta start somewhere, so this is the place to get your competitive ball rolling.

The two-day tournament recurs over Fridays and Saturdays, and follows the standard ruleset (which you can check out in detail from Epic Games). Hype Nite is intended to act as an entry point for any player hoping to play competitively, so hey, what are you waiting for? Time to get hype!

TIP:

Even if you don't see yourself as the next Ninja, there's no harm in dabbling in a little competitive play. The Arena serves a metric to measure your skill against other players, but you can also just use it as a fun way to play matches against players of a similar level.

FORTNITE CHAMPION SERIES (FNCS)

Those who work their way up the competitive ranks are eligible for the FNCS, the seasonal cadence of Fortnite. FNCS are the real deal, with cash prizes on the line for top-ranking competitors. At the seasonal launch of Chapter 1, Epic gave away a total of $5,000,000 in prizes across a range of regions and competitions, from weekly Cash Cups to platform-specific tournaments like the PlayStation 4 Celebration Cup.

Remember, if you're not keen to take part, you can still catch a lot of the FNCS action on the official Fortnite Twitch channel, where they stream FNCS finals. You can even earn special event drops for your trouble.

LOOKING TO THE FUTURE

It's impossible to know what lies ahead (and 2020 certainly proved it's somewhat futile to even try) but Epic is hopeful that it will be able to return to large, offline events sooner rather than later. They expressed a desire to host another World Cup event in 2021, so hey, time will tell...

THE FACES OF FORTNITE

The sources of Fortnite's success are long and varied, and while it obviously helps that the game itself is a banger, a huge chunk of its unwavering popularity and prevalence in the gaming scene has to be attributed to its streaming presence, and the big personalities that keep it one of the most watched games online.

The pro players of Fortnite stream the game and create content across a wide range of platforms, regularly raking in the viewers and raising the game's profile while also taking the time to teach their audience a thing or two. If you want to be the best, you've got to learn from the best, and when it comes to Fortnite, these faces are the best of the best.

NINJA

What's a Faces of Fortnite list without Tyler 'Ninja' Blevins right at the top? Ninja has been synonymous with Fortnite since the game's launch, and his popularity hasn't faltered - even after a controversial platform switch from Twitch to Mixer.

2020 was a big year for Ninja Fortnite-wise, as he became the first creator to receive his very own official in-game skin. Considering the work he's done in building the online community, he was the perfect pick to kick off the game's new Icon Series, with the Ninja Outfit, Ninja's Edge Back Bling, Ninja Style Emote and Dual Katanas Pickaxe debuting back in January.

WHERE TO WATCH:

• YouTube

WATCH FOR:

High-paced, aggressive playstyle and FPS mechanic flexing.

BUGHA

When it comes to choosing a creator to watch, does the reigning Fortnite World Champion require any real persuasion? Kyle 'Bugha' Giersdorf shot to Fortnite stardom in 2019 when he won the Solo Fortnite World Cup Finals, taking home the title and a sweet $3,000,000.

Without the World Cup in 2020, Bugha has been keeping busy with appearances in other competitive tournaments, like the NFL Streamer Bowl. He streams regularly (a mainstay within Twitch's Top 10 most viewed Fortnite streamers) and also uploads highlights to his YouTube channel for viewers that can't catch him live.

WHERE TO WATCH:

- Twitch+
- YouTube

WATCH FOR:
Powerful shooting and building techniques.

NICK EH 30

Watching Fortnite is all fun and games until someone gets on the wrong end of a lucky shot and tilts off of the face of the earth, and that's where Nicolas 'Nick Eh 30' Amyoony's positive vibes and smiles come in.

Interestingly, Nick was well-known for making content for solo action-adventure games like the Last of Us and Uncharted before making the switch to Fortnite, which is when he started blowing up. His Fortnite content landed him a big deal with Twitch just after Ninja left the platform, filling the vacuum for family-friendly but still fiercely competitive gameplay.

WHERE TO WATCH:

- Twitch
- YouTube

WATCH FOR:
High skill, PG-style gameplay and positivity.

CLIX

There's room for people of all ages in Fortnite content creation, and Cody 'Clix' Conrod is one of the youngest big names on the scene, having been born in 2005.

Clix is a regular fixture on Twitch, often within the platform's monthly Top 3 watched Fortnite streamers. While he regularly qualifies for competitive tournaments (including 2019's World Cup; a feat Ninja couldn't pull off), he's yet to put a big win to his name, but his recent win at the NFL Streamer Bowl and his youth and skill definitely mark him as one to watch on the scene.

WHERE TO WATCH:

- Twitch
- YouTube

NICKMERCS

PCs aren't for everyone, and while the vast majority of the online community plays on PC, Nick 'NICKMERCS' Kolcheff is one of the few who caters for the console gamers out there, without sacrificing any skill.

NICKMERCS' YouTube channel is a must for any console players, as it is a treasure trove knowledge base full of educational videos and stream highlights. If you're playing with a controller, you need to know NICKMERCS.

WHERE TO WATCH:

- Twitch
- YouTube

WATCH FOR:
High energy and skilled, evolving gameplay.

WATCH FOR:
Unbeatable console gameplay.

TFUE

Turner 'Tfue' Tenney is arguably Fortnite's King of Twitch, raking in the big numbers (around 20k live viewers per stream) while still retaining a competitive edge for years, widely regarded as one of the best Fortnite players in the world.

Tfue may be a more controversial figure in the community, but he also consistently delivers crazy, exciting gameplay, particularly in Solo matches. While he may be somewhat unpredictable on stream, he still has skill for days that's not to be missed, so... viewer discretion advised?

WHERE TO WATCH:

- Twitch
- YouTube

TIMTHETATMAN

Sometimes pro play can get a little intense, which is why it's nice to kick back and have a laugh with streamers like Tim 'TimTheTatman' Betar. TimtheTatman is a variety streamer, but Fortnite's a definite favorite of his, and a frequent feature on his channel.

But don't count him out because he focuses on entertainment - Tim has some serious credentials with FPS skills and mechanics from CS:GO and the likes under his belt as he leaps out of the Battle Bus, ready for action.

WHERE TO WATCH:

- Twitch
- YouTube

WATCH FOR:
Thrilling, high-octane gameplay.

WATCH FOR:
Fun gameplay with a focus on entertainment.

QUIZ ANSWERS

Check your answers from the survival quiz (p. 44-45) and add up your total score to find out where you place in the true Battle Royale: game knowledge.

1. A –0, B –3, C –1, D –0

2. A –3, B –1, C –2, D –0

3. A –0, B –-1, C –0, D –3

4. A –2, B–0, C –3, D –1

5. A –3, B –1, C –0, C –0

6. A –2, B –1, C –3, D –0

7. A –0, B –3, C –1, D –2

8. A –0, B –2, C –3, D –1

9. A –3, B –2, C –1, D –0

10. A –0, B –0, C –3, D –0

11. A –0, B –2, C –3, D –0

RESULTS

0-9 POINTS: YOU PLACED #100 -#75

Okay,so... the only place to go is up, right? Your fundamentals are still lacking, so maybe review the material a few more times if you want to aim for that victory royale.

10-18 POINTS: YOU PLACED #74 -#50

Not too shabby -you have a basic understanding of the game and will likely survive the initial landing massacre, but there's a good chance you'll find yourself in trouble in later stages of the game when faced with more enduring survival challenges. If you want to make it further, brush up on your build knowledge and healing priorities.

19-27 POINTS: YOU PLACED #49 -#25

You're on your way to becoming a force to be reckoned with. You can survive the landing scrimmage, you can build up your loadout and survive the majority of duels you come across -but the devil's in the detail when it comes to Fortnite, and there are a few that are still eluding you. To get Top 25, you'll need to familiarise yourself with the finer details of Fortnite, like the numbers. You've got this.

28-33 POINTS: YOU PLACED TOP 25!

Well, well, well -how does it feel to be as lethal as a point-blank shotgun headshot? You know your way around that map, around your resources and around any obstacle that may fall in your path. The only thing standing between you and a Victory Royale are other players with the same knowledge mastery. So how can you get the edge if you know the info just as well? Practice. It'll make perfect, after all. Review, reinforce, and pick out your favorite dance emote to break it out on top of No.2's corpse when you cinch that Victory Royale. No harm in being prepared.